DEVIL WORSHIP

Devil Worship

ALL IS ABHORRENT FROM THE WRONG PERSPECTIVE

Liv McCaughey

Daniel Buck

Wobbly Cat Creations

If you think you may be sensitive to any topics covered in this book, please don't hesitate to flick to the back of the book and consult the trigger warnings before reading

For Santa-Claus Minotaur - kitten, grandma, bebe

Jack-o-Lantern

(a letter to the reader)

Lighting up from the inside
is your gift
in-spite of the life
you are living,
the face you did not choose,
that does not belong to you
like the flames in your irises do
If you feel doused in suspicion
while the Wicked rest, dry
- the pyre they gather
never caught on... fire
Recall, you are strongest
where least wanted,
brightest in the shadows
of others, you are not immune
to propaganda, in the spiral
of a spiral **Exorcisms In Your Area**
How To Be Myself   But Less
But Better   festers.
Death to indifference
All is abhorrent
from the wrong perspective -
Decline the exorcism
or resent it

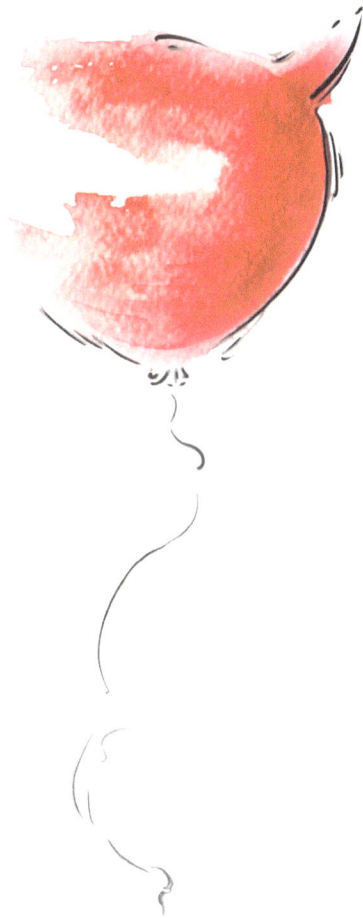

Our Jimmy

Our Jimmy never cared for school
but has a voice like thunder,
Our Jimmy never went to uni,
was never no boy-wonder

but has taken quite an interest
"*Gossip makes myths hips look fact*"
and he's a bit of a bastard but
he's our good Jimmy lad!

Jimmy gets to the truth
even at a push, Jimmy gets his fact
from fiction, from TV and Facebook
I says back-up those sources

He says I only have HP
and we all laugh a belly laugh, now,
that's our Jimmy! They try to
put him down, to shut him up

He doesn't give a ****
takes no notice, they're all jealous
if he has a thought he's sharing it
in a declarative - sharpening

weapons (of mass-misinformation)
people try to drown him out
It really doesn't phase him
voice of a generation -

they say, Jimmy saved them

that he's a modern Malcolm X
but they're seeking out their
own enslavement

*"Under the skin is where they keep
the cursed objects"* He said before
pulling out a fiver and sampling
some ***

An Invention

The most magnificent creation
since the immaculate conception
The greatest vision since television
most beloved and ambitious
The best thing since sliced bread,
cutting edge, et-cetera
never been done, thought
or said before, I wanted **nobody**
to take it seriously, I wanted **nobody**
to take it from me, so, I wrapped it up
in pink and gave it to a teenage girl to safe-keep

The Scariest Movies Ever Made

were documentaries,
Evil was ordinary
No orchestra kept score
Bad was worse
than you
could imagine,
Nobody guides you
by the hand,
Tells you what to feel
and when to scream

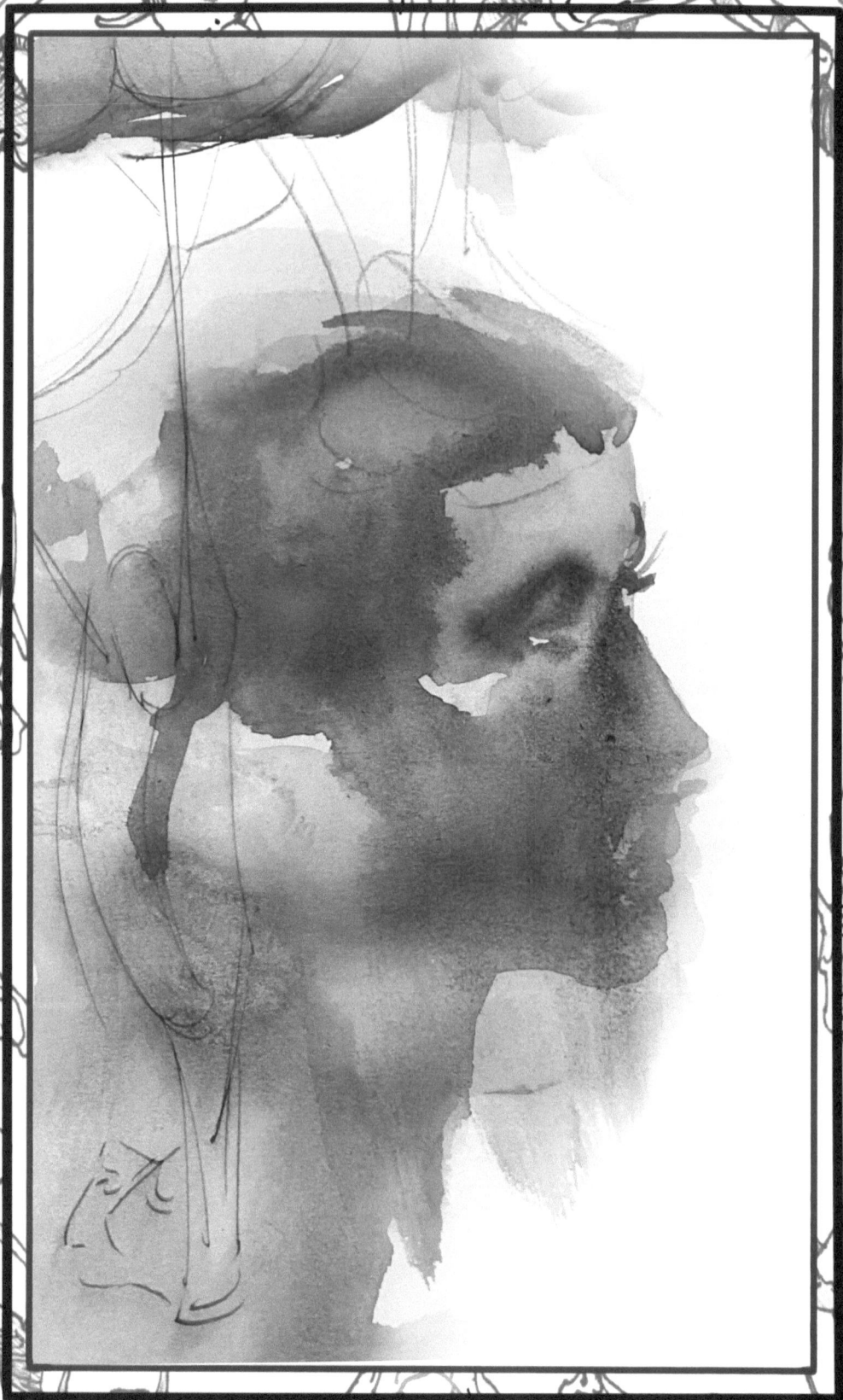

Ode To The Kid I Killed

Life uncovered
from the rubble
from a sentence
carried in a casket,
wondering
when over is
and how much
longer 'til we
get there

Brought to you
by the funeral-song
I chose at fifteen
that chokes me
to this day -
the light behind
your eyes
carries on
I wouldn't change you
for the world

but I'll skip you
forever
French hydrangeas
for veins
Belladonna to sleep
I used to
break like china plates
Fine set in concrete

as a shatter
happens
to me,
I crumple

Fallen flower
never-green,
out of view
of sun, buried
in mud
                stuck
my legs held
hidden
messages back then
- I far from treasure
mapped out skin,
Strawberry Milkshake
in the bathtub

and Raspberry Blitzed
to the hips
but they called it
as they saw it
Teenage nonsense
or *attention-*
seeking bullshit
from an ungrateful
bitch

Endless Afternoon

I exchange compliments with
the shampoo bottles
They break my rose-quartz heart,
crack my skin, sting
my scalp, vacant promises drip
and laugh tracks
splash the bath-mat, lazing,
bathing, nothing is changing
except for the squishy squashy
body that has risen
like fresh bread, like coffee foam,
I wear clothes so big - old ladies
say they swallow me, if drowning
is the silent exit, this is the vessel
for it - Ophelia looks like she is sleeping
with her crown above the water,
dreaming, a mundane spirit slaughter

I Had A Spiritual Awakening

but I am still a jerk
I lived long enough
and became the enemy,
as heroic as Batman
if he ran for
the conservative-party
and I was a fuckboy
with your feelings
Intolerant as your stomach
Prickly as your worst lover
despite this green tea,
meditation, nature walks,
TED talks, reiki (I'm kidding
I haven't studied reiki yet)
I am still an asshole
(sometimes) not at heart
should this be
an autopsy
your long limbs,
wind-chimes
in melody meet
reverberating
through the cave
of my self-inflicted
- loneliness
and I curse music
for existing
in the first place

Don't Piss Off The Almighty!

Aphrodite, creamy as the cake
they want to eat
So let them eat and choke
and blame
the Goddess for the ripples
on temporary bodies
For sugar and for honey, for-only
consolation-prize smiles
Spring won't come without the presence
of the Empress even-if the world
still blames her for winter

We're Going On A Bear-Hunt

(after Michael Rosen)

Life began to feel like hard-work and thoughts
unwanted relatives on the drive after tea-time
'til a few years back, life could be surmised to
one sentiment **something to get over**
to trudge through

We can't go under it or over it, we will have to
go through - on a bear-hunt without a trap
only open-arms, a chest holding back
panic, not scared but **unprepared**
for neverland found

Hundred acre woods pillaged for firewood, life
isn't good like we thought, growing up
the sugar is taxed so I won't coat it **sanity**
is a full time job for some
Going on a bear-hunt

with no weapon is better
than wasting **at home**

A Memorial in Malta

there are no words
all I have are letters
I can't use correctly
Words which meaning
would not reach
the knee of tragedy
         - no words only
crumpled paper, pathetic
attempts at solace, but there
are no words for it

Love As A Graveyard

Knows the body well
is peaceful, lays
meadow flowers
Embraces the earth
and rests in blackbirds
calls and in owls twit
-twoos tried to read
the ending, prematurely
all I got were paper-cuts
nothing stings quite
like them

I Used To Fall Asleep To True Crime Podcasts

I used to be tougher and harder to bludgeon. What happened?
Then   a girl   curious...
Researching The Art of not being a Dead Girl
How to NOT GET RAPED

Alongside hot-topics; classics since ankle skirts
How to SLEEP AT NIGHT led to dead ends

Meeting dawn in blue light
avoiding dark alleys, free drinks, your drinks,
walking, talking - *aggressively*, whatever

that could mean {insertamillionotherthings}
Come back to update this list daily, living too boldly
Walking across the street unconscious to the moment
I can't tell the blood from my ears, from the dye on my head
Now   a woman   awake
wincing at the mention of murder, the lazy policing, the girls
on the corner, the boys from bad families, mutilated -
bodies, contaminated evidence, the marginalised
with nobody left asking questions - how am I
both desensitised and still *too sensitive?*
I turn it off and try to dream of things
that have not happened yet

The Underworld Is Not Hell

(for Hades) it is home, call him God of Death to his face

He only corrects you on his bad days when she's left to

tend to spring - in good spirits for Halloween, he was

hardly - heartless *if* it matters to the angry mob he was

agreeable, said he and Lucifer get along

he has *nothingbadtosayabouthim* that familiar yarn,

I hate to play Devil's advocate (but) *he was nice* (to me)

quando a Roma, to the locals, barbecuing bitches in Hellfire is culture

Thirteen Before It Gets Its Teeth

Corridor leaning dolly-daydreamer's
The pair of us press buttons on an LG Cookie
and I'm in the background of all of the selfies
on your DSi XL, hair teased to heaven, screech
like hell if the cubs forgot their place - we tossed them
back as a mercy, verbally we get violent,
reared on Mean Girls, Wild Child, High School Musical
circa 2007, looking to the villains for some ambition
Sharpay Evans deserved better

You think what I think
if someone dies
will you help me -
bury the body?
You are the only person
who understands
me

Playground Pasta King discourse covering
Saturday-night TV, it always seemed to rain
and we were made to stand outside
- the wittiest kids that ever lived, best forever
friends, little women projecting what they see
on screen, all the teens are played by 20 somethings
We pick apart our bodies
like the vegetables
we won't eat

and that's thirteen *before*
it gets its teeth, *before*
Sophie drinks Slim-Fast for breakfast
and we all wish on a fading star that we could
- cut our stomach with scissors, have magazine
-figures, collage as someone different, not too dissimilar
to the work we'll get when we're women

After the last bell rings in, doll-hearts breaking in
rotation, kaleidoscope of cut throat, big girl bodies
breaking in, remember the sensation of
laughing, lying on the trampoline,
planning big city lives 'cause
we hate small towns, wait
'til we're out

Now
we stay
(in touch like a thread caught/
                /doesn't tell me much but I let go/
                  /I do not pull you off/ you still have
who i am in the palm of your hand/ because of
who i was)

We don't speak but once wanted to share
a fish-tank sink, wiping rain from your
iPhone 3G, cracked-screen, just wait
'til we're eighteen
We'll leave, move to NYC and live
in an apartment like they do on FRIENDS
Why not? Anything can happen
(at thirteen)

People Disappoint Me

decomposing, slowly
already compost
                        and you are afraid to die ?

Good For Her!

Bella doesn't wake up
in perfect makeup
Bella stopped being that kind of girl
When camera's came to a grinding halt
The film faded as the earth warmed up

It finally *clicked* when rogue is in vogue
they'll call her *ahead of the time* but for now,
she is not well liked,
Bella is the next Megan Fox

They say Bella is the Megan Fox
that Megan Fox never was, never will be
and Bella is
burning bridges with cars on-top

Towers fall with every step,
no foresight and no empathy
like a superhero movie
- Infrastructure crumbles in her wake

Bella doesn't look the same since
she only plays Mommy cooking up
breakfast for the family
to leave - untouched

is it because she's a terrible mother?
or because
her husband is
running late, honey

He has to rush off
to the main plot,
a script is a script, the budget
got cut, the list went black and goes on :

She became difficult to work with,
toxic vibes on-set
8 times Bella was a total bitch!
They believe anything spoon-fed
to them

The special effects, that she is a natural
- redhead but not that inequality exists
anymore, how's that for ungrateful?
You wouldn't steal a handbag, so

Why steal the show? She won't
stop acting-out in public, destructive
and disruptive
Latex skin and rubber nipples

Heaven-sent or demon - ?
She never needed her own movie
If you ask the internet - yeah, she hexes
in her perspex but if we were being

True to the *original comics*
original vision she'd have less
character development and
larger breasts

Good For Her (The Sequel)

Fight like a grrrrl. Be the hero of your own story
You can't spell Girlboss without I or money without
me (machine) what's current is the currency, cracker men
paper money
She bats her lashes, teases tornadoes and you will only
ever watch her go — get one for your home; a t-shirt,
an action figure, lunch-boxes, a wet-dream (of a late-stage
capitalist) Press- release to a sequel of a box office hit,
a cult classic, *how did you do it? How did you get so slim-thick?*
Superhuman, do the curtains match the cape?
What do you eat in a day? Hard as bricks with small tits,
how do you stay so confident? Are you a woman,
a weapon or less?

Maneki-Neko

I used to have friends
They stabbed me in the back
So, thank GOD that I have cats

SSR-SIGH

I'll build a mountain out of a mishap
Celebrate mistakes you make in memory-foam
Genetically short, trying to grow, I don't
mean to spread my roots over to you, it is as easy to do
as my nature, as forgetting once and waking up in this body,
constantly

I go where you go, you go to the toilet
I doom-scroll on my phone, a toothpick to discontentment
- we are shopping for a Hallmark holiday and our show
was cancelled so we drank bottles of Prosecco in Soho
with no objective

I hold your hand across the table, I'll never be
stable, will that ever sink in ? My turtle-neck chafes,
I retreat into my shell before agitation
rattles my bones like heavy metal,
and all you wanted was brunch

                          in the corner of my eye, see you
watching me - lose my shit

The people of the city crawl around like millipedes
and I can smell the shit on the streets of London
Did I tell you? The dream that I had
- we went swimming in our underwear
I sat poolside writing poems about forgetting
my tablets pulled the towel from my bag
out fell my prescription, I fall victim
to myself

I'm A Crying Baby On An Aeroplane

at best you feel bad for me,
I find it hard to articulate my rage,
shove it in your face , gently
Pretty, crying baby, disappointing
like a watery orange, a once appealing
peach spoiling, ruining the whole
Fucking Fruit Farm
the catchy cult of Baby Shark,
Yogurt fingers on a scratched iPad,
the stench in the room, the fart,
the poo, the screaming baby on an aeroplane

I Wish I Was Daphne But I'm Probably Shaggy

Zoinks! Invite the things that scare me
out for tea or watch them show up uninvited
to my nightmares, jumpscares behind retina screens
in REM with no RSVP, the ghost train
to the haunted house becomes
a right of passage, as the trees
are passing, under lantern

light, all-aboard my midnight train
of thought, 7 pieces of carry on luggage,
sweat out what has been, release
myself from other people
(s conscience) this was supposed to be fun,
Solving mysteries at what cost to us?
I'm not scared like I was

Open the dungeons, lets jet-off to Spooky Island,
Feel afraid, go even though "Spooky" is in the name
Treat myself to Scooby Snacks, wear lilac
go-go boots to kick - the door down
Let's split up, look for clues and look
cute doing it

I have transformed my body into a
dangerous weapon, the antagonist to
the oppressor, the woman I was
made better, all of your choices
are sending you

somewhere,
where are you going?
Now who's the damsel in
distress? If bad guys wear the skin
of friends, don't flinch, don't fear
their real face, pinch yourself
and end the dream

They would've gotten away with it too
If it wasn't for you

I Went To Hell And All I Got Was Sweaty

Songs he'll screw your boyfriend to on a loop
(as above, so below) blow in a genderless bathroom,
damned to (smoke) static from the radio, communication
limited to subliminal messages (experimentation with)
reversed records, so they say they're passive-aggressive
System of a Down to Britney Spears. Toxic baby
cant you see? I'm calling, can't call him callous
for carving, the name circumstance left him
onto life's pumpkin, ripening, rotting, not
reigniting a halo reduced to an echo
or picking a scab, stubbing it out,
his pleasure is the next distaste,
dad-dancing on stage, pretty lame
but who am I to judge ? nitroglycerine
in the thick of it, too hot,
thick skin, peels off. who I was gone - still someone
His reputation (era) precedes, warms the seats,
he was nice to me, we're in the Riot place at the Right time
usually, paved a party scene, from just another villain
to chillin' and killin' for a living, chains hang
from his Y2k denim, *I'm so different,*
screw tradition, no asthma in the afterlife
He bummed me (smokes) all-night

The Undressing Of Venus

As with most atrocities unfolded over time
Aphrodite birthed in seafoam ; the product
of sexual violence, stands naked in the living
room of a rapist

The year 2000, *not much has changed*
except they live under the cover of **Feminist**
Good guys never have to advocate their goodness
Pray they don't

- **darken** that they never pick you
four-leaf clover - of misfortune, she watches him sleep,
cum and go with the good girl quiet
of an inanimate object

Botticelli ceramic, keeps eye-contact
Has a body sculpted for her, he takes
a beer from the fridge, adjusts the bust
on the mantle (with hands he never washes)

Misremembers his legends, she is a meddler,
did Pompeii pray to her or know better,
than to admire, gold and barbed wire?
Both and neither, silence is the most sacred *thing*

he keeps more stolen relics
than the bowels
of the British Museum

I Am Just Like Other Girls

I bleed pumpkin spice,

                                             I can't drive

I just squeal in an annoying high pitched voice

I am just like other girls,

                                    stupid, basic

bitch

        I paint my face,

                                I comb my hair

I cry to Taylor Swift

Satanic Panic

Hidden in the television
lookin for bodies for possessin'
souls to rot
test subjects to shush
doing the most damage
that can be done by
existence alone
or less than
culture cracked
like a **Monster** can
brainwash 666
comin' for the kids,
takes the image
of the under-
represented
Neighbourhood
watcher watches,
sees what they want to see
; emo poetry, a Judas
Priest E.P, calls the police
but *first* does their own research
Identifies weeds
in flower-beds
from books they read
or at-least from looking
at the pictures ---
Critical thinking
withers in the distance
Poison only
works if ingested
Thorns stuck in

hands, they bleed
and we will
grow back

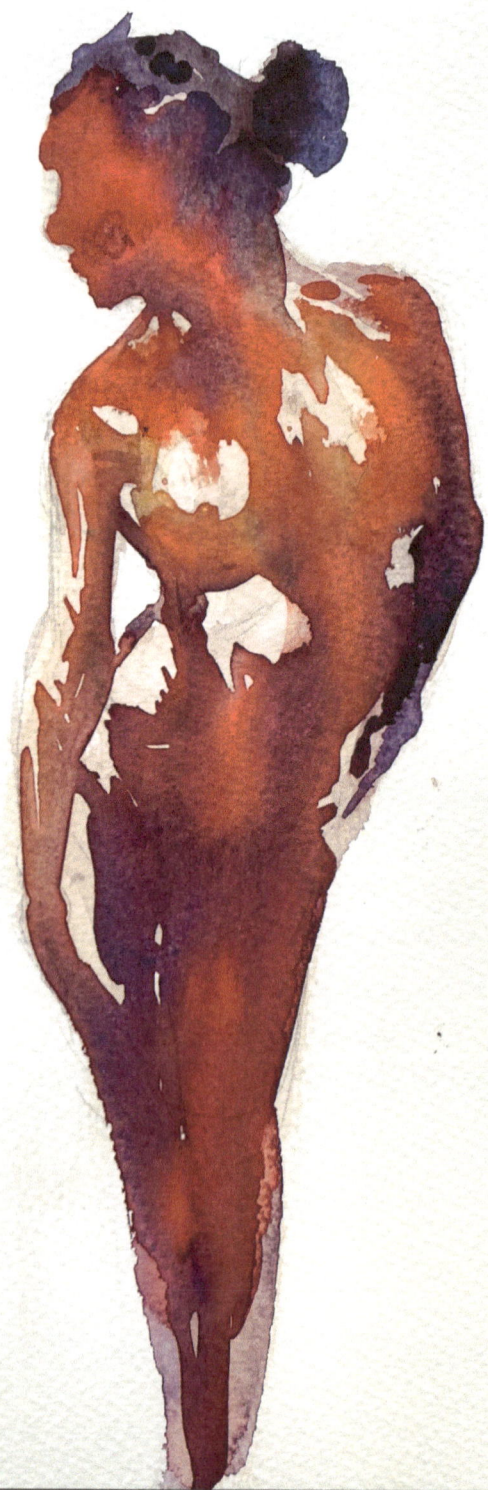

Devil In Disguise

Your chaos can be the place I stay
when I grow tired of muted red
and grey, I think of you and recall
dreams of crumbling teeth, glass inside
the buttercream, Chelsea smiling, crimson
wedding, early-morning, without the church
or the blessing, blue from borrowing loyalties
and worrying

The great grandfather (of generational curses)
will be in attendance, cause a disturbance
on my big day gives a speech "in memory
of when we were menacing" I stick out like
an objection and don't dare to dream any different
He's hell bent on never finishing anything, so
he doesn't start to end, he lives life
as one big speculation

Pleasure having tried its best to share the scent
of happiness, found time and time again
Its flowers were false, disregarded
the evidence, he said *if*
you love me enough,
you will birth hell
like a baby and
you will raise it as your own!

Pain

The chambers listen
in your heartbreak
hotel-suite
feeling nothing
as a family
the smoke at best
gives your lungs
a 60's feel
and your pride
something to hide
in, the language we knew
fell out of use, the game
collects dust on the shelf
in my room,
my teenage time-capsule
paralyses with posters
already down
Fanaticism peeled
from me like
the magazines, the walls
Violin skin in swan song,
wearing reaper rags
to curtain call

And Other Creatures

I have some hellish features and I saw them in your looking glass

You took yourself for granted and did your best to try (I hope)

did less and less to stay alive (I know) if this was the wild,

you would lay down to die, but it is not, I do not fall far from

the tree but keep rolling onto something -

Creamy Cuntentment

Days like today are satin to touch
Life is namely named for living
with love, creamy-cuntentment
slippery when wet, that's what she
said, up at night alluding to a good time,
skinny-dipping in the minds of people
who don't like me, white wine
spritz, starlight on my eyelashes
Lightening from my lips, doing the things
they ask for but hate to see, I try my best
to be utterly unaccommodating

I love being   a girl   not always
behaving, how they'd like, I don't mind
being hard to pin down, to cull
with a look hard to miss and fire
hard to kill, they say I am unladylike
I don't fit in - to their narrative
so be it

Everyone's perception is distorted by their own
clouded skies and murky water, I ride
the tide to my next place
in the world

Waitress Woes

I am aggressive when I say shit
like I'm Sorry I'm Not Interested
I'm Sorry But I'm Working
Thank You For The Specific
Comment On My Appearance,
Thanks For The Offer but I'll pass
on that, at my best learning thank-you
for the compliment won't cut it
at my unluckiest, apologise
for being my(usual-dry)self
Add it to the tab, I'll pay for that
For he has assumed a person
I will never be and is not pleased
with the trickery that is
my personality, I am too big
for such a small body
Too bold, too loud, too comfy
and I'll pay for that too
For being rude, for not
smiling as you drag
your shoes and if I'm balanced
- soon, faces flush the same
like I am crazed and if I am pretty
- soon, I will only be vain,
to be put in my place by
who better than you? and I'll pay
for that too -

Iconoclast

There is mud traipsed in
like a crime-scene
you can find her, glamorised
poison-ivy never lying
in wait, climbing
restless up a temple
lush with orchards, orchids
blossom, doves coo and
the wind chimes in

Call me divine or nothing
She need not look at you
Renaissance painting
presents herself
and you avert your gaze,
tempted they'll have told her
in the way without words
Over-time warm skin
untraceable, far beneath
cool marble, she is suspended
over her earthly home

A gargoyle, naked and
wont wear the shame
they give
           or worse
fade in
   to the architecture
Not a liar, a convincing
fake

There's A Blue Tit At The Grocery Store

and every baby will be born in the future, so
I will never be
a baby

My birthday would be embarrassing,
stopwatch tickling feet
"there is time"

and so many *things you can do,* so many
things you can see, *every second of*
every day

doesn't have to be suffocating
There is a blue tit at
the grocery store,

living off of apples, I can do
what I want, whenever
I like, the door

is there to go
Outside

Rose, Lavender, Chamomile

burn of my lip-plumper
or sting of the roger heart-shaped glasses,
rose-tinted lenses, cotton candy
clouds, bubblegum gunning for oblivion,
when I am inside, the rain is
so beautiful - and when I'm outside
too, if shelter waits patiently like a mother
at a birthday party, counting to ten, time is relative,
spell it out in this instance 1 2 3 I don't know
if anyone will understand the life I want to lead
or appreciate it but I am learning it is possible (and
magnificent) to ignore it

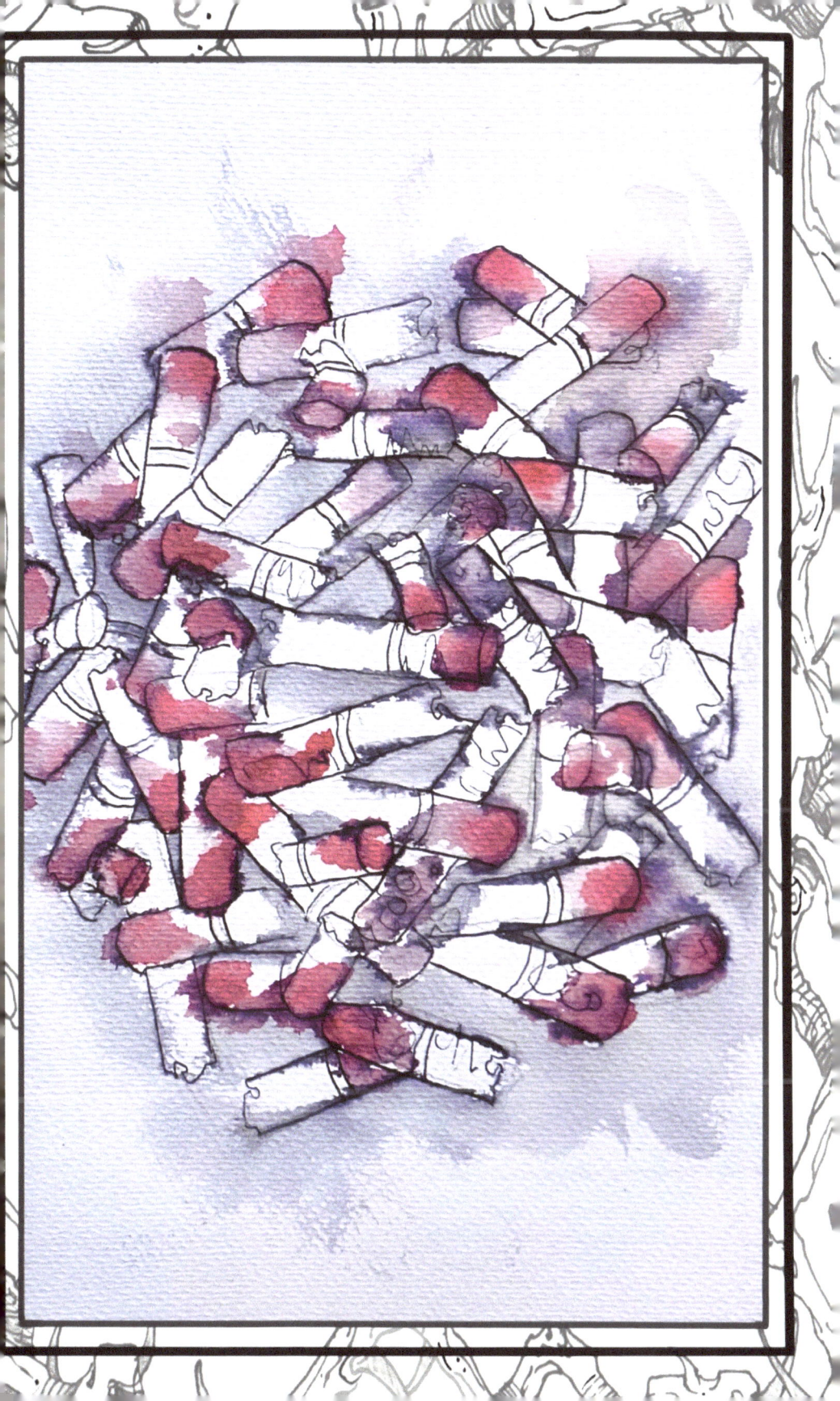

The Torture Of The Artist
(After Van Gogh)

Begins with fridge-freezer masterpieces
and ends with their darlings killing them
Everafter, **everything is chaos** simply-put
to exist in cellular bodies : **me me me**
holding a gun to my head, that's a wrap
the potential in plastic - **suffocated**
trying to keep fresh, to make content,
to stay relevant, people cross the street in avoidance
like/ **"I have put my heart and soul into my work
and I have lost my mind in the process"**
/ you're Van Gogh, never know
praise or compensation for
an overactive imagination, live in it
instead, lie to the second, they're first
and the only - but you're only lonely
Squirm and make nothing
worth **consuming**

Nobody loves an artist more
than they love the Art, the process, the focus,
Make them choose between the two,
bring nothing but cold and rain,
a vitamin d deficiency, a mood disorder
possibly, say n*obody likes their poetry*
and leave - them to it in a windowless room,
with a half-empty glass, where nobody
can clap or cheer

Wonderland

He calls me forest fairy, says **this body is
a porcelain-dreamscape, I must be dreaming
like the dead do, just to love you**, the mad
interrupt - anticipating contrariwise, he waits
for me to finish, our brains wired different
High up in Heaven, down in Wonderland,
where you don't shrink me or think me mad

Eat me, grow big on a mushroom bed
with enough space for tea for two,
an eternity of off-beat crockery,
outside, wild as weeds,
you and I and no screens -

He looks at me, and says he **sees
right through thechaosIconsume**
I say *I love you too* to the hollowed out tree
I've moved into /a tree like him/ with arms like his/
called me his/ and I became the leaves on his branches,
I fell with the breeze, from high up in Heaven,
down to Wonderland

After Largo

(by Fiona Apple)

I don't know what I'm hoping for
I pull the Devil on Valentines
and it's been swords ever-since
Damned or blessed by the things
- that go bump in the night,
not sure why I try or would
ever give it up, for
beginners luck, all on black,
it has been nothing but

- swords and signs I can't read,
the passing of time, happens to me
but I cannot bare watching her leave,
give me new scenery, I could
reminisce purgatory if you gave me chance to
think in romantics and put in the legwork,
stir my own pretty soul just fine, on my own

In my comfortable company, *doing my thing*
Stick my best in a book for my eyes only
Haveeverymemoryoverwith let this eternity come to its end
- written in gel pen, password lock for these thoughts
of spin 'round the drive if I stir this cup, three times,
clockwise, it's my party so, I'll drink alone

Call your phone in the AM but Do Not Disturb
I leave - after the beep, love letters to the city,
to the buildings that fell down on me, I pull
the Devil on Valentines day and sleep in
a rose-petal bed of my own making

Sensory Overload Brought To You By Hearing A Bee, Seeing A Sound And Knowing Nobody Wants Me (Around)

tongue, unattended told its secrets with a sour face

sealing fate, the weakness is hive in mind

crystallized in freak-out, two too many

sounds, colours, voices, creepy crawlies, trail

my aura, eat my rotting words and smother

the butterflies in my stomach, die feeling something

with a rumble, come to the honey again, I won't

blame you yet, for abandonment, for leaving me

half-cooked human, dumb-dead to shed my bed,

clear the attic of my bolted head for more self

-loathing, less faith in beauty, serenity, anything

having any meaning, intrusive voices

voiceless if we just trust

in the honey again

I Do Not Remember

November 2nd so bright, crisp as
still as this morning in the dew,
crouched in the archway, a bird calls,
it was no song, it was shrill and
reset everything

Happy Birthday To My Heartache

to the blood on my shoe and to you
the sound of slamming doors
the wolf blew shut, happy birthday to my scars,
you made it this far, straightener burned
thigh, finger trapped in a car door

dancing on the bar, cheeks peek
beneath my skirt, Happy birthday
to my self-respect, to all the boys I've hurt;
I send bouquets to their mothers
with handwritten notes, condolences

perfume sprayed, wrapped up in the present
condolences, wrapped up in the present
Happy birthday the card reads **You had it coming**
Buckfast sounds like success if you have begun
slurring, begging is no burden so **Happy birthday**

to my heartache, I'll bite my cake
with candles lit, pour a double for
myself and the rest of it
down the drain
Toast sobriety,

the after-party is still going...

GUTTED
like a November pumpkin
waiting for the end

A Bit Much

but who doesn't
love
a sugar rush
who wants to
hear
their favourite song
at volume one, only
a couple of stars
to scatter the night
swept up in storm
disregard (I am)
the sky
I'll likely ruffle feathers,
don't hold your breath
if I am too much
go find
less

What Time Were You Born?

You don't talk about your feelings much
I am an audio-book, or was
You don't care for muck
for me, for poetry, monogamy
or the bands I bankrupt myself to see
at eighteen, we listen in your car, go
go nowhere, you don't care for me
then and don't fool me now

All I do is too woohoo for you, libra man
why ask me about the moon?
knowing you I never knew peace
(do people feel the same about me?)
Justice looks the other way, only monsters
text after midnight
Do you know your birth time?
I've been trying to explain
how it is you are that way

If the stars have a say why not
let me see? Is it too late to ask
for the chart? It can't be - on your lips
like sticky toffee, miles away,
hearts apart, hungry, humming
a lullaby only I sing -
Ask after him half-hoping
for a vacancy or expiration

Typing a memoir
only I see
You don't talk about
your feelings 'til you're talking
to me, may we find peace
at the opposite ends
of the universe

Far enough apart to balance
each-others bullshit
The only ours to start with
We could still support each-other
All we gotta do is
avoid each-other
All I know is Fiona Apple
and your avoidant
attachment style

You remember everything
sepia, peachy, manic
and dreamy
You've taken a sabbatical
to madness, extended
the invite but can't
take me
with you

I am not the magic woman
- *spelling* life out for you,
I cannot smile for you
  Poof

Acknowledgements

Finally she's here! A quick start and a slow finish. From the moment I knew I wanted to create this collection and what the title would be, I knew that I'd potentially lose some people along the way, or before even giving it a shot, if you made it all the way here then congratulations, you've done the opposite! So firstly, I'd like to apologize to any of the older generation of my family/relatives for the scare, I hope you can appreciate that this is a meaningful work and was based in far more than just edginess. That goes for Mum Mum, Nanny and Granddad, I love you! Sorry as always I have to be doing the most.

I'd like to thank Callum Wensley for their continued mentorship, for editing this book and consistently pushing me to be my best, even when I hate you for it. (okay not hate just severely cringe at my being percieved) I would not be here releasing my second book today without you and your wisdom I am evergrateful to have you in my life. Thank you to Kathryn O'Driscoll for the few sweet times we've spent together and all the unwavering support you have shown me ever since. Thank you Cal and Kathryn for really making me feel a part of a community.

Thank you to my Dadager for having the answer to almost every question I have and always being on the other side of the phone to fix my problems or offer solutions. I am so happy with the time I got to spend with you all in the Yorkshire Dales and the space it gave me to focus on my craft and make a controversially titled book... ta da! love ya!

Mum, I know how excited you have been for not just this book, but anything I've ever made. It's easy to take that for granted when you are used to it. But I never in a million years doubt your love or belief in me. You are my biggest fan and I love you so much, thank you for raising me to appreciate art and poetry from all different walks of life.

Daniel, thank you for bringing this collection to life again. You have always said I was going to do great things, but I love that we are doing the great things together. The book could not exist without you, it's as much representative of your endless creativity as it is any of mine. It's amazing to look back on our work and see how much we've grown, let's keep at it! And thank-you dear reader! Thank you to anyone that has ever read my work or encouraged my writing, it has always meant so much more to me than I can describe.

About the Author

Liv McCaughey is a poet, actor and tarot reader from the UK. Since winning the first **BBC Radio 2 500 words competition** at 12 years old, McCaughey studied at university in Bristol where she performed at local events, developing her spoken word voice and writing her debut collection **The Southside of Doubt** - which would go on to make the Amazon Hot New Releases list. Liv takes part in multiple creative pursuits and has acquired some accolades so far, including reaching the 2019 **LYRA festival** slam-final, working with *Paper Nations* over their Great Margin project and performing at **BBC Bristol**. This is Liv's second self-published poetry collection and she plans to diversify into other styles of writing next as well as working with other writers on their self-publishing journey. You can keep up to date with Liv McCaughey and her upcoming projects on Facebook, TikTok and Instagram at **@theunpoeticpoet**

About the Artist

Daniel Buck is a tattoo artist, illustrator and painter from the UK. He is currently based in the south of England. He earned a first class honours degree in Drawing and Print from the University of The West of England, receiving rewards of achievement for his dedication to the course. Daniel has been tattooing for a few years and now works as a Junior Artist in Manhattan Ink Aylesbury. He enjoys all artistic pursuits and illustrated Liv's first book. He has also worked with the BBC on projects such as, *Life Drawing Live with Lachlan Goudie.* This book was illustrated directly from Buck's interpretation of the written work, this is their second book together and they look forward to collaborating on more work in the years to come. You can keep up with Daniel, particularly his tattooing on Instagram at **@13triplesix**

Trigger Warnings

Mental Health

Self-Harm/ Suggested/ Ode To The Kid I Killed, Thirteen Before
It Gets Its Teeth

Suicide Ideation/ Implied/ Ode To The Kid I Killed

Scars/ Mentioned/ Happy Birthday to My Heartache

Substance Abuse/ Suggested/ Happy Birthday, After Largo

Eating Disorders/ Implied/ Thirteen Before It Gets Its Teeth

Violence and Death

Violence Against Women/ Implied/ The Undressing of Venus, I
Used To Fall Asleep To True
Crime Podcasts

Rape/ Mentioned/ I Used To Fall Asleep To True Crime Podcasts,
The Undressing of Venus

Rape Culture/ Implied/ The Underworld is Not Hell, Waitress
Woes, The Undressing of Venus, Good
For Her!, Good For Her the sequel

Death/ Mentioned/ Pain, And Other Creatures